This Doodle By Number
Belongs To

....

By Doodle Lovely

Flowers always make people better, happier, and more helpful; they are sunshine, food and medicine for the soul.

LUTHER BURBANK

TWEET! BUZZ!

There's nothing lovelier than doodling down the garden path.

Doodle By Number™ isn't just for kids, it's for anyone who wants to quiet their busy thoughts, awaken their creative spirit, and enjoy the peace that comes with a little mindfulness.

And what better focus for a mindful activity than the fresh flora and friendly fauna that flourish in our gardens.

Gorgeous gardens welcome us to slow down, breathe deeply and stop to smell the roses. That's why I designed this book: blooms and doodling are a natural fit, and we could all benefit from more of both.

You don't need to be an artist or an expert to enjoy doodling. You just need to start moving your pen across the paper, ready to follow the journey wherever it may lead.

Wishing you a fresh & fragrant day of doodles,

Melissa x

WHY DOODLE?

It's true! People have been doodling for millennia.
"Spontaneous drawing" has been studied and verified as a
means to decrease stress in our lives.

Taking pen in hand and using the rhythmic motions of doodling, activates
the relaxation response within the brain. Just the thing to calm the chaos!

Playfulness
Doodling promotes
well-being, allowing you to
lighten your mood whenever
you feel overwhelmed.

Creative Freedom
Doodling is a workout
for the mind that can help
you focus on new ideas and
bring fresh insights.

Improved Focus
Doodling is a simple and
effective way to help you
concentrate and process
information.

DISCOVER
THE BENEFITS
OF DOODLING
TODAY

Manage Emotions
Doodling is a safe method
to evaluate unsettling
emotions, converting jumbled
feelings into a peaceful
state of mind.

Greater Productivity
Doodling can refresh your
mind and reset your thoughts,
allowing for a greater
sense of clarity.

Increased Memory
Studies indicate that while
listening to others, the brain
can recall 29% more
information while doodling.

How to use your
DOODLE by NUMBER™

Pick up a pen, your favorite marker, or pencil of any color.

At the bottom of each example page there is a selection of five doodle patterns to choose from. Each pattern is circled and numbered.

Follow the numbers to create a doodle pattern on the opposite page. If you want to use more or less doodles, go for it!

Complete the *Doodle By Number*™ and touch it up to your satisfaction.

Feel free to make the doodle your own with your favorite shapes, lines and patterns. Even add color if you like. Doodle-riffic!

Follow the numbers to match your doodles on the opposite page.

1 - Scallops   2 - Antennas   3 - Swirls   4 - Circles   5 - Lines

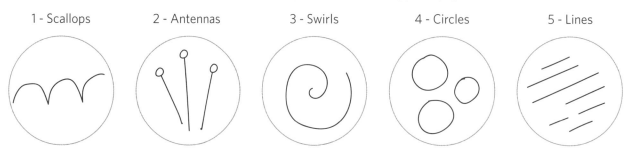

Happiness held
is the seed;
happiness shared
is the flower.

JOHN HARRIGAN

Follow the numbers to match your doodles on the opposite page.

1 - Tents

2 - Swirls

3 - Ovals

4 - Lines

5 - Scallops & Strokes

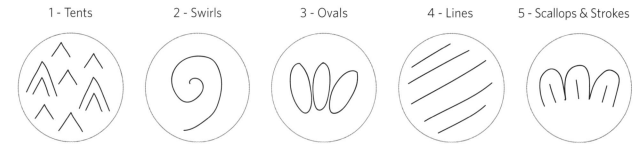

The flower
that follows the
sun does so even
on cloudy days.

ROBERT LEIGHTON

Follow the numbers to match your doodles on the opposite page.

1 - Stars   2 - Sprinkles   3 - Wavy Lines   4 - Circles   5 - Swirls

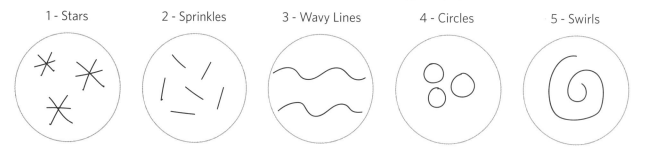

Wherever life
plants you, bloom
with grace.

UNKNOWN

Follow the numbers to match your doodles on the opposite page.

1 - Squares   2 - Wavy Lines & Dots   3 - Bird Tracks   4 - Sun Beams   5 - Lines & Strokes

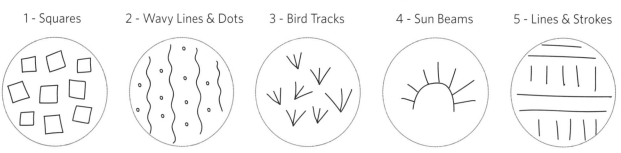

Learning never
exhausts the mind.

LEONARDO DA VINCI

Follow the numbers to match your doodles on the opposite page.

1 - Scallops 2 - Antennas 3 - Scallops 4 - Bird Tracks 5 - Lines

   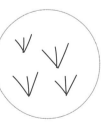 

*I must always
have flowers, always,
always, always.*

MONET

Follow the numbers to match your doodles on the opposite page.

1 - Wheel Designs   2 - Square Spirals   3 - Swirls   4 - Stars   5 - Lines

   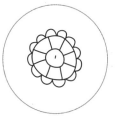 

Flowers are
like friends;
they bring
color to your
world.

OSCAR WILDE

Follow the numbers to match your doodles on the opposite page.

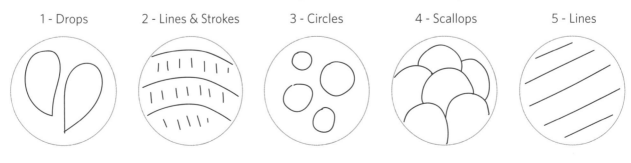

1 - Drops 2 - Lines & Strokes 3 - Circles 4 - Scallops 5 - Lines

If you look the right way,
you can see that the whole
world is a garden.

FRANCES HODGSON BURNETT

Follow the numbers to match your doodles on the opposite page.

1 - Ripples   2 - Squiggles   3 - Tear Drops   4 - Circles   5 - Lines

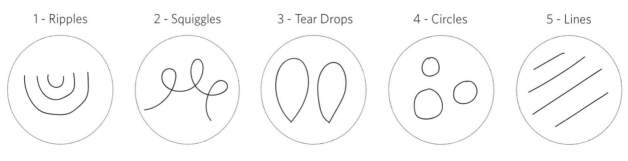

All the flowers of the tomorrows are in the seeds of today.

INDIAN PROVERB

Follow the numbers to match your doodles on the opposite page.

1 - Circles   2 - Triangles & Circles   3 - Sprinkles   4 - Wavy Lines   5 - Scallops & Strokes

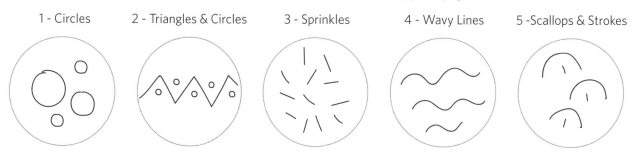

A flower does not think of competing with the flower next to it. It just blooms.

ZEN SHIN

Follow the numbers to match your doodles on the opposite page.

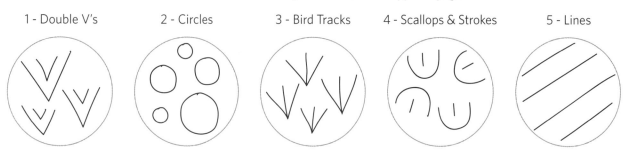

1 - Double V's   2 - Circles   3 - Bird Tracks   4 - Scallops & Strokes   5 - Lines

Every flower
must grow
through dirt.

LAURIE JEAN SENNOTT

Follow the numbers to match your doodles on the opposite page.

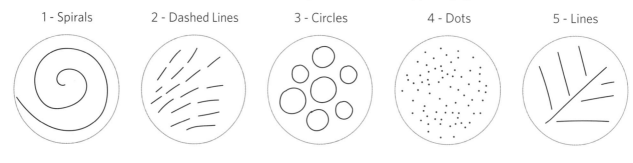

1 - Spirals 2 - Dashed Lines 3 - Circles 4 - Dots 5 - Lines

Take time to smell the roses.
PROVERB

Follow the numbers to match your doodles on the opposite page.

1 - Scallops & Strokes   2 - Circles   3 - Lines   4 - Antennas   5 - Lines

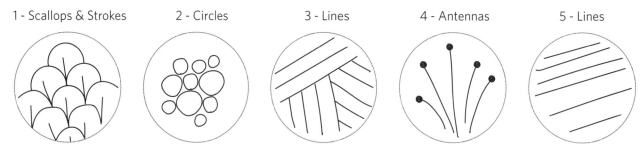

Love is the
flower you've got
to let grow.

JOHN LENNON

Follow the numbers to match your doodles on the opposite page.

1 - Fuzzy Spirals   2 - Circles   3 - Stroke Zigzags   4 - Full Dots   5 - Lines

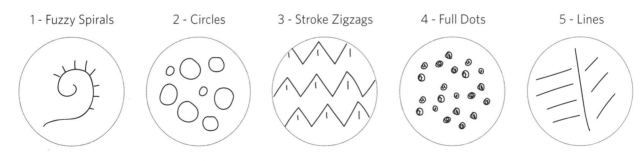

Anyone who has
time for drama is not
gardening enough.

AUTHOR UNKNOWN

Follow the numbers to match your doodles on the opposite page.

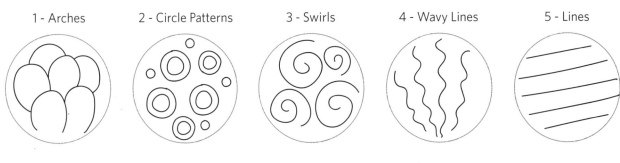

1 - Arches   2 - Circle Patterns   3 - Swirls   4 - Wavy Lines   5 - Lines

Bloom where you
are planted.

UNKNOWN

Follow the numbers to match your doodles on the opposite page.

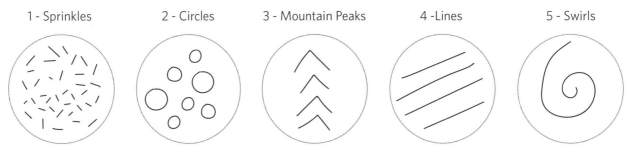

1 - Sprinkles   2 - Circles   3 - Mountain Peaks   4 - Lines   5 - Swirls

Smile, breathe
and go slowly.

THICH NHÂT HANH

Follow the numbers to match your doodles on the opposite page.

1 - Circles   2 - Lines   3 - Sprinkles   4 - Wavy Lines   5 - Dots

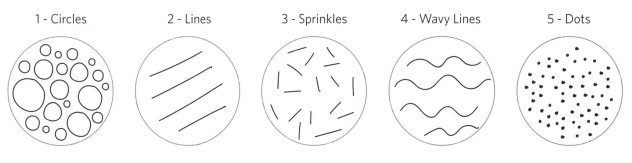

Every flower
blooms in its
own time.

KEN PETTI

Follow the numbers to match your doodles on the opposite page.

1 - Circles & Waves   2 - Rounded Lines   3 - Full Dots   4 - Strokes   5 - Wavy Branches

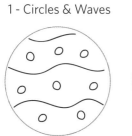    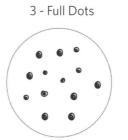

She is like a
wildflower;
beautiful,
fierce, and
free.

UNKNOWN

Follow the numbers to match your doodles on the opposite page.

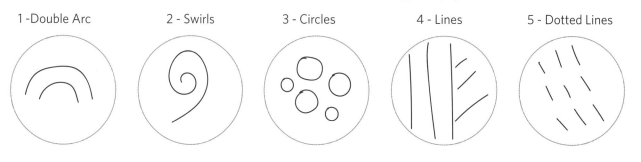

1 - Double Arc   2 - Swirls   3 - Circles   4 - Lines   5 - Dotted Lines

Do something
today that will
encourage you
to blossom.

UNKNOWN

Follow the numbers to match your doodles on the opposite page.

1 - X's   2 - Mini Rainbows   3 - Circles   4 - Lines   5 - Scallops

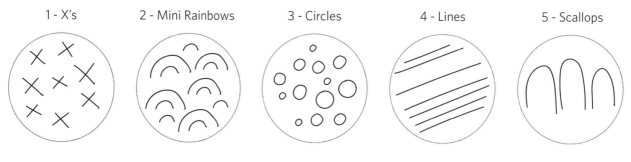

Politeness is the
flower of humanity.

JOSEPH JOUBERT

Follow the numbers to match your doodles on the opposite page.

1 - Circles & Dots   2 - Waves & Strokes   3 - Swirls   4 - Arches   5 - Lines

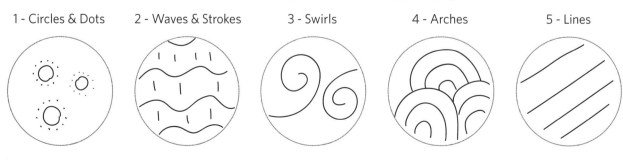

Plant a seed so your
soul will grow.

HAFIZ

Follow the numbers to match your doodles on the opposite page.

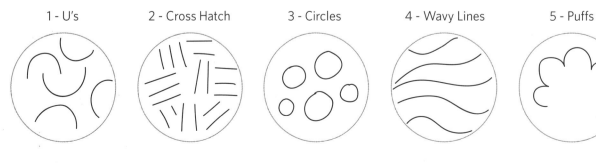

1 - U's   2 - Cross Hatch   3 - Circles   4 - Wavy Lines   5 - Puffs

Let your
dreams
blossom.

UNKNOWN

Follow the numbers to match your doodles on the opposite page.

1 - Circles & Dots   2 - Antennas   3 - Puffs   4 - Peaks & Strokes   5 - Lines

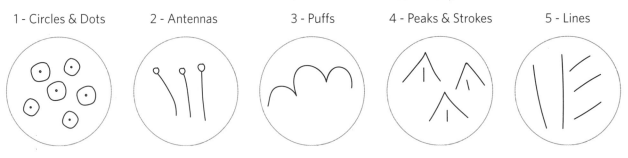

Don't forget to
water your dreams.

RIHANNA

Follow the numbers to match your doodles on the opposite page.

1 - Fuzzy Circles	2 - Basket Weave	3 - Snakes & Dots	4 - Swirls	5 - Checkers

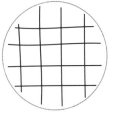

The earth
laughs in
flowers.

RALPH WALDO EMERSON

Follow the numbers to match your doodles on the opposite page.

1 - Tear Drops   2 - Zigzags & Circles   3 - Wavy Lines   4 - Squiggles   5 - Stars

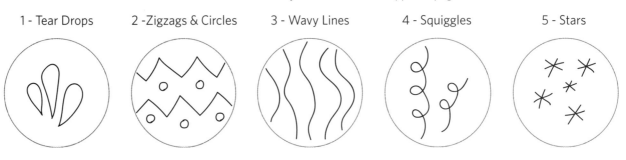

Flowers don't tell,
they show.

STEPHANIE SKEEM

Follow the numbers to match your doodles on the opposite page.

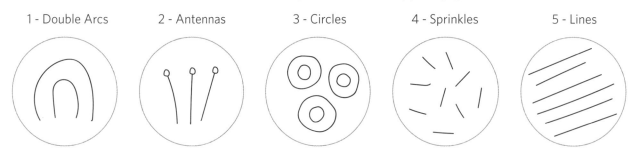

1 - Double Arcs   2 - Antennas   3 - Circles   4 - Sprinkles   5 - Lines

Happiness
blooms from
within.

UNKNOWN

Follow the numbers to match your doodles on the opposite page.

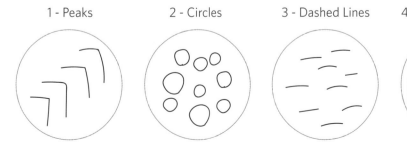

1 - Peaks   2 - Circles   3 - Dashed Lines   4 - Arcs & Strokes   5 - Lines

Don't wait for someone to
bring you flowers. Plant your
own garden and decorate
your own soul.

MARIO QUINTANA

Follow the numbers to match your doodles on the opposite page.

1 - Triple Arcs   2 - Circles   3 - Antennas   4 - Lines   5 - Waves & Circles

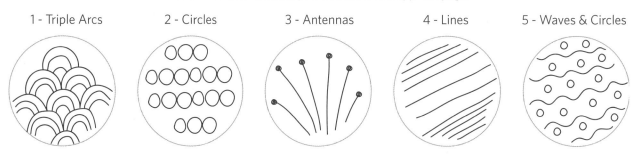

To plant a garden
is to believe in
tomorrow.

AUDREY HEPBURN

Follow the numbers to match your doodles on the opposite page.

1 - Circles   2 - Sprinkles   3 - Swirls   4 - Wavy Lines   5 - Lines

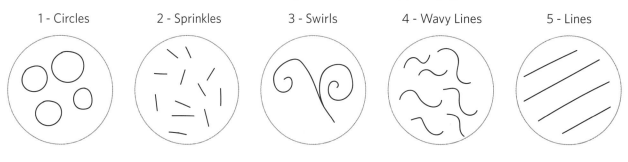

Be honest,
be nice, be a
flower not
a weed.

AARON NEVILLE

Follow the numbers to match your doodles on the opposite page.

1 - Zigzags   2 - Lines   3 - X's   4 - Arcs   5 - Circles

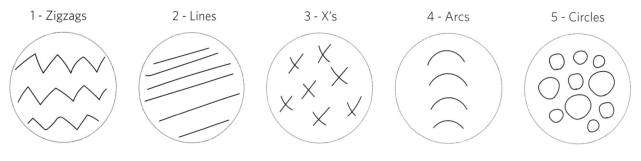

A flower
blossoms for
its own joy.

OSCAR WILDE

Follow the numbers to match your doodles on the opposite page.

1 - Double Arches   2 - Triangles   3 - Dots   4 - X's   5 - Lines

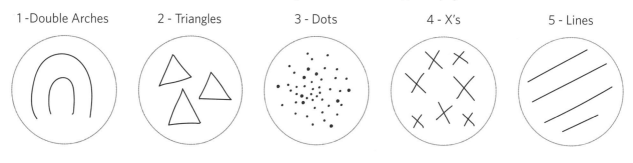

Do something
today that will
encourage you
to blossom.

UNKNOWN

Meet the Doodler

MELISSA LLOYD is an international doodler, designer,
teacher, author and inspirationalist. Her passion for
creativity can be found globally on products, environments
and in the hearts of those with whom she has connected.

Melissa combines her twenty plus years of experience
in professional design and communication with her passion
for humanity, psychology, art therapy and mindfulness;
infusing a deep understanding of self.

Melissa teaches soul-care through creative practices and
encourages you to learn how to navigate the stormy seas of life,
reducing stress and rejuvenating your mind.

By honoring your creative soul and the celebration of
living in the moment, Melissa inspires you to bring joy back
into your life by finding a place of peace internally.
Her transformational approach to creativity, through doodling
and living, inspires others to live a healthier and happier life.
'Always Be You... For You.'

Melissa balances her time between mothering, creating,
teaching and living in her little Cottage By The Sea.
To discover more of Melissa's work visit: **DoodleLovely.com**

DOODLE Lovely™

Let the beauty of what you love be what you do.

RUMI

Did you enjoy this *Doodle By Number*™? We would love to hear your feedback!
Please email us: **hello@doodlelovely.com**

Connect with us to know when the next edition of *Doodle By Number*™
will be available in our online shop.
www.DoodleLovely.com

IN THE DOODLE LOVELY WEB SHOP

Doodling to calm the chaos

Doodle Lovely is here to provide soul-care through
creative products so you can live a healthier and happier life.
See some of the other titles in this series below.

BEGINNER - DOODLE BY NUMBER™ SERIES

Beginner Doodle By Number™ - Volume 1

Beginner Doodle By Number™ - For Dog Lovers - Volume 2

Beginner Doodle By Number™ - For Cat Lovers - Volume 3

Beginner Doodle By Number™ - For Botanical Lovers - Volume 4

Beginner Doodle By Number™ - For Holiday Lovers - Volume 5

These and other titles are available from the Doodle Lovely Web Shop.
www.DoodleLovely.com